Gasari's Herd

Written by Caitlin Fraser

Illustrated by Meredith Thomas

Flying Start
to Literacy®

Contents

Chapter 1: Gasari the brave

Many years ago, an elephant was born.

This elephant was adventurous and brave and she was much loved by the rest of her herd. She was not scared of anything!

The herd named her Gasari because Gasari means fearless and brave.

When Gasari was young, she was always exploring. She would walk away from her herd and discover parts of the jungle that she had never seen before. She liked to see other elephants that belonged to different herds.

As Gasari grew, she began to leave her herd for longer and longer and she would walk further and further into the jungle.

Chapter 2: Gasari's despair

One day Gasari walked a long, long way from her herd. When she came back to her herd, she saw people with guns and nets.

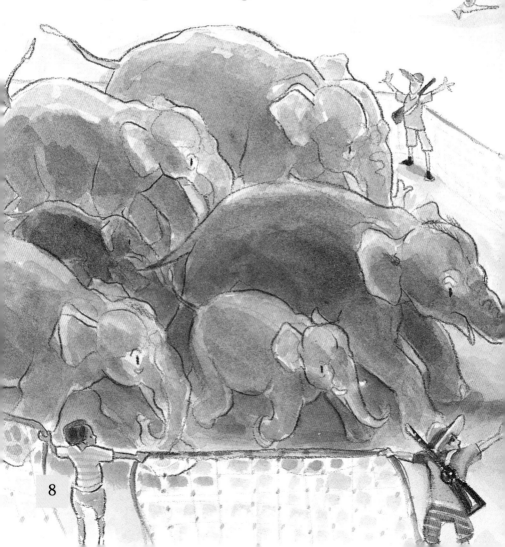

The people pushed all the elephants in Gasari's herd onto big trucks and took them away.

Gasari watched from behind some trees. There was nothing she could do.

Gasari tried to find her herd,
but she did not find them.
She looked for them everywhere,
day after day, week after week.
She became tired, sad and lonely.

Gasari knew that she would never see
her herd again.

11

Chapter 3: A brave rescue

Gasari went to the river to think.
What would she do?
Where would she go?
How would she survive by herself?

When Gasari looked up, she saw
a little elephant standing by the river.

Then Gasari saw a lion creeping through the grass with his eyes fixed on the little elephant. The lion sprang towards the little elephant with its mouth wide open.

But brave Gasari leaped across the river and pushed the little elephant out of the way just as the lion's teeth went "snap!" The lion crept into the grass.

The little elephant was so frightened
that it ran back into the bushes
and out of sight.

Gasari felt sad as she watched
the elephant go.

Chapter 4: Gasari's new herd

As Gasari turned to leave the river, the little elephant returned with a herd of elephants.

At first, Gasari backed away because she was frightened. But the elephants were friendly. They were thankful that Gasari had saved the little elephant. They came closer to Gasari because they wanted her to join their herd.

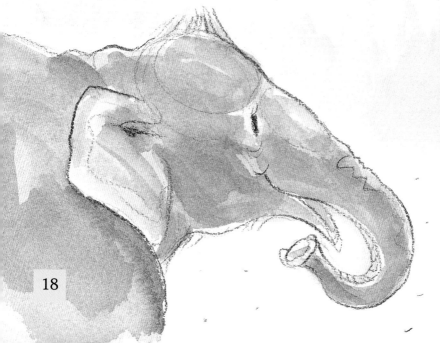

Now Gasari is part of a new herd
of elephants. She helps her new herd
by looking after the little elephants.
She helps them to stay close to the herd.

Chapter 5:
Gasari the happy!

Gasari is happy again. But she still misses her old herd. She often thinks about them and wonders where they are.

A note from the author

I once watched a documentary on the life of elephants and I was amazed at how close the elephant herd is. At one point in the documentary, one of the elephant calves died and the anguish shown by the mother and the other female elephants was heartrending. The mother even cried real tears.

This inspired me to wonder what would happen to an elephant that did not have a herd to take care of it. Elephants, just like people, need a "herd" to belong to. And this is where I got the idea for the story of brave Gasari.